In the spring of 1969 on the outskirts of Torremolinos on the Costa del Sol in Spain, a young photographer, Paul Carter, came across a small blue van. It was home to the Whitfield family who were passing through on their journey around Europe. Over a few days he took photos of the family, the local people living and working around them, the tourists and the new high rise apartments.

The photos document a moment in time, a crossing of ways between wanderers. They anticipate the changes in the air for the family and for Spain.

A Moment in Time - SPAIN 1969

Paul Carter and the Whitfields

Paul Carter Publishing

Paul - How I met the Whitfields

Spain, early March 1969. I was young and footloose, wandering about Europe with my Leicas, building a portfolio of photos which I hoped would kick-start my career as a photographer. A week or so before, I had celebrated my 21st birthday by being ill in bed with flu in the dormitory of the Barcelona youth hostel. I thought I might feel better if I headed to the warmer south. I decided not to hitch-hike this time and jumped on a very slow but very cheap train to Malaga instead.

My spirits picked up when I got to Malaga and I started to explore. One day while I was on the lookout for pictures, a man, an American if I remember rightly, came up to me and asked if I was OK. I was surprised, for as far as I could judge I was feeling quite content, apart from itching a bit from the bed bugs that infested the mattress in the pension where I was staying. It turned out the chap was a vicar who was just making sure that no young people passing through Malaga were in distress.

The conversation lead to where I was staying, and it ended up with him getting me a place to sleep for nearly free on a sofa in a new high rise apartment block that was let out cheaply to groups of travelers during the winter. It was in Torremolinos, a short bus ride from Malaga.

Torremolinos was once a quiet fishing village, but in 1969 it was making its mark as a major tourist destination. A forest of apartment blocks was beginning to grow along its open beaches. It wasn't exactly the Spain I had in mind to photograph, but I started to get excited about the clash of old and new.

One day, as I was taking pictures of the developments, I came upon a little blue van parked on the edge of a building site near the sea. Beside it stood a man painting at an easel set in the dust.

The van was the family home of the Whitfields. There was Bryan from Yorkshire, his wife Catherine from Dublin and three young children. They had been on the road for nearly two years and were pausing in Torremolinos to earn a little cash.

The Whitfields welcomed me aboard and let me take pictures of their daily lives. Although Bryan worked regularly and seriously at his painting, the general atmosphere around the family was one of relaxation and simplicity, one moment flowing easily into the next.

I came to admire how they had found a way to live life on their own terms. "Being together" was the most important thing to them. They could pretty well just following their instincts. I especially loved seeing the children spill out of the van and on to the beach, living each second as it came. It all seemed so perfect.

Yet it felt a little fragile too. The cranes on the construction sites spoke of change. It was the end of the sixties. Nothing was going to be quite the same - neither for Torremolinos nor for the family. The Whitfields were camped in the middle of what was to become a busy beach road. But at the time, the future didn't matter to any of us.

Catherine - How we came to be in Torremolinos

After Bryan saw Jean Luc Goddard's film *Pierre Le Fou* he made a note in his sketchpad to buy a van. It sounded like a good idea to me. Bryan started to work nights and we saved. We eventually bought a second hand one in Brixton in 1966 - an Austin J2M16 - aluminium body, custom built interior, insulated with fiberglass and lined with plywood.

The next year we decided to leave London and go on the road with the children - Mason (aged 1), Emma (aged 2) and Josephine (aged 3). It seemed the most natural thing in the world to do.

By the time we met Paul in Torremolinos, we had been travelling for almost two years and were at ease with our lifestyle. We gave little thought to the future. Our clothes were sent to the nearest Post Restante from my family's "Basement Boutique" in Dublin, hence the 60s style. The children were happy, self-sufficient and free.

While we were away, England was changing it seemed. We started to meet long haired people seeking a new way of life. In Morocco we came across Suzi Creamcheese of Frank Zappa fame and Hoppi who had been involved in the alternative paper IT. The Rolling Stones played Hyde Park, but we were going our own way. I am glad we made the journey. It was liberating.

We did encounter some disapproval, though I am reluctant to give that sentiment credence because the experience was life enhancing and romantic. Being a family made our encounters simpler for many reasons. Firstly people like children. We had that in common and we had to be responsible and interact with others. That was a pleasure.

We did not give much thought to the implications of all the new apartment blocks we had parked beside in Torremolinos, the beginnings of the Costa del Sol as it is known today. The buildings represented the future but we were blissfully living in the moment. Paul saw this contrast of life styles - the tourists, the fishermen, the shepherds and our little van.

Although he took these photos over a few days in just one of our stopovers, they somehow represent the whole journey we made from autumn 1967 to late 1969. The photographs are a precious reminder of a formative and adventurous chapter in our lives and on a wider level they are a timeless portrait of youth, freedom and change. They capture fleeting moments and are symbolic of the adventure we had as a family. They epitomize the 1960s when everything seemed possible.

Catherine - Life on the Road

We only had about £100, so working to pay our way was essential. This enriched the experience and meant we had to be more involved in life on the road.

It was a joy to unfold the paper maps and plot a route through France. Bryan drove, I was the navigator and the children sat in the hammock just behind the cab. We headed south and the first place we stayed for more than one night was in a campsite in Madrid. We met an international crowd of people, enjoyed the swimming pool and made trips to the Prado. I usually stayed outside in the beautiful cool garden with the children while Bryan visited the museum. I saw some boys playing bullfighting in the dusty park, one being the bull and the other using his coat like a matador. Bryan sold his first painting of the trip. It was a small landscape.

Leaving the beautiful city we drove south. On a rocky road diversion, outside Seville a spring broke. We made it to a garage where they fashioned a new metal plate to replace the one that had cracked. We stayed in a hotel for a couple of nights. We felt lost without our van, but we never thought of giving up. There was always a way of solving a problem. If the battery went flat, we had a crank start. Some vehicles made in 1966 still had that option.

The engine never let us down in spite of once filling up with diesel by mistake. The answer to that was to keep filling up with petrol and not to stop until there was no more black smoke from the exhaust. The roads were quieter. It was before motorways.

May in Spain was perfect. We stopped at a small feria in the woods. It was like a scene from a Goya painting (a rural scene) - children on a rope swing, dancing, kite flying and a bodega set up under a tree.

There was no work in Spain so we decided to go to Gibraltar. That was complicated as there was no road access from Spain. Spending the last of our money we took the van on the ferry via Ceuta to North Africa and then came back to Gibraltar via a ferry from there.

Arriving in Gibraltar the customs demanded a surety of £70. That was a lot of money, so for the one and only time on the trip I had to ask my parents to send some cash, which of course they did. Thinking back now I realize we never got the money back when we left.

Gibraltar was like a small English town but in the sun. We parked by the beach. In the heat of the day the children used to have a siesta in the shade of the van. They were at ease and had each other.

One day we were summoned to the frontier where, to my surprise, we found my 15 year old brother Patrick waiting. He had arrived penniless, having been robbed on his way through Spain. He found us by describing who he had come to see and they discovered us easily by the beach. Pedestrians could pass into Gibraltar so they let him in and he stayed for a few weeks, sleeping on the beach.

Kindness played a great part in our journey. For instance the German manageress in the casino where I first worked in Gibralter happened to meet us in the park and seeing that we had three children doubled my wages. Bryan became manager in the same casino for a while.

Later I worked in a nightclub. I loved watching the cabaret acts. It wasn't like working. I still remember the flamenco dancer swirling around with flashing eyes.

By this time Bryan was running a bar in the centre of town. That is where he met some Americans who offered him a job working on a boat in Agadir in Morocco. They were looking for oil and needed crew.

A Moroccan friend called Suli came with us from Gibraltar to Tangier. He showed us around the city. It was wonderful, so different to Europe. It was our first time in Africa. There were oranges and watermelons piled up for sale on the roadside. The narrow streets of the casbah were full of activity.

Not surprisingly our van got caught on a protruding metal sign, so after that we had a distinguishing taped up patch. It worked well - no leak - but later nuts fell from a tree and made a crack in the perspex roof which was awkward in the rainy season.

We had our first taste of Moroccan hospitality in the house of Suli's sister. Sitting around a low table, we ate spicy chicken with prunes and couscous. I do believe that you learn about friendship and the importance of sharing good food when you have that sort of experience. Suli accompanied us to the edge of the city where we said goodbye and set off south towards Agadir.

Sometimes we stopped on the road and Bryan painted. We stayed in Agadir for six months. Bryan was well paid by the Americans. The campsite was next to the beach but the Atlantic waves were treacherous. I almost drowned there once.

That winter we met lots of travelers - an American on his way home from Vietnam, some other Californians who sang "Come On Baby Light My Fire" all night long (they had come to surf), Dutch ex-conscripts who were now at liberty to travel and create havoc, an Italian couple who made mayonnaise in their camper van and many others. All the vans were of a moderate size. Huge camper vans did not exist then.

The Moroccan people we met were generous and friendly. We were invited into their homes and once had the privilege of being the guests of the Blue people who lived in tents at the edge of the desert. We had given one of the men a lift back after he had failed to find work in town. They considered using our camping gas but rejected it in favour of their usual open fire. So we had another delicious meal. As guests we were offered the best bits of meat.

Christmas 1967 we spent on the beach with friends. First we brought the live chickens from the market in the van. Then we prepared them for our homemade barbecue. The people of the town gave us boxes of small sweet mandarins. On Christmas day a troupe of acrobats appeared from nowhere to entertain our motley crew.

At the market we ate delicious spicy fish, drank mint tea and banana milkshakes. The women liked the children and gave them treats as we wandered round the market. This is where we bought our large earthenware plate to share our meals on the rest of the trip. The children had their little plastic plates.

Then we moved on. We had two fellow travelers on the journey north. They were Londoners. When we ran out of petrol on a remote mountainous road they haggled so much the garage refused to give us any fuel. I had to intervene and apologise so we could continue our journey to Spain.

We heard that there was a small town called Rota where there was an American base and we could find work. There was always somewhere to park and live. We stopped near the sand dunes. This is where we found fig trees growing in the wild. Katinka, a little girl whose father was attached to the base, befriended the children and gave us gifts of food and the cowboy boots Josephine is wearing in the photos.

I worked in one of the many bars with spanish girls. The customers were American sailors. They drove wide american cars around the narrow streets of Rota and never swam in the sea. They considered it too polluted. We survived our daily dips. Then the time came to leave, restlessness I suppose.

It was Easter when we drove into Seville. The streets were full of people watching the great procession. Hooded figures and men carrying crucifixes filled the streets. We were in the heart of Spain. I spoke enough Spanish to get by so I worked in a bar once again. At that time all the customers were men. The women stayed home. Franco was still in charge then.

During the day we camped in an orange grove. The oranges were the bitter sort suitable for making marmalade or feeding to the pigs. It was a lovely shady place for the children to play and Bryan had plenty to paint.

In the evening we drove to the centre of town and parked near the bar where I worked. One night there was an earth tremor and we woke in the morning to find some people had left town. After that we were careful where we parked. Everywhere we stayed was memorable yet at the time it was just part of our life.

When we arrived in Torremolinos we found an ideal place to park at the edge of town. We often had the beach to ourselves, especially at twilight. By then Mason was 3, Emma 4 and Josephine 5 - old enough to enjoy running on the beach, sitting in their little breeze block cafe and amusing themselves. We had few possessions in the van. There was no need. We had sunshine.

How the easel and all the paintings fitted in is a mystery. I worked with girls from all over Europe in one of the many bars in town. It was fun. Living in the van meant we could move on any time and were not tied down by paying rent in an apartment. Bryan looked after the children and painted. He still paints and I still cut his hair.

There was no time scale to our journey. The van was our home. We had no other and we had no grand plan. We decided to head for France to pick grapes. It was hot as we drove north towards Cordoba and then on to Toledo. It was a feast day and everything was closed. We had to wait a few days to see the paintings of El Greco. Then we headed east through the beautiful Spanish interior towards the coast. Bryan painted small pictures of spanish dancers and I went from cafe to cafe selling them. We earned enough to buy food and petrol to carry on.

Work was plentiful in France and we spent weeks living in idyllic country settings picking grapes. Later we picked olives near Arles on an old estate. We parked near the chateau. All the other workers lived in the barn nearby. We had fresh peppers and all the salad we could eat not to mention wine. The barn was a great party venue for all of us workers. Roget, a Belgian ex racing cyclist, travelled with us for a while. He slept in the front cab. He was not only very entertaining but was good at persuading the vineyard owners to let himself and Bryan sample all the best wine in their cellars.

In the Autumn of 1969 we drove north to Amsterdam. The city was vibrant. We stayed for a short time, parked by the canal. It was a great experience but we knew it was time to move on. We headed back to England. It was a little sad when we eventually sold the van but by then we were living on a narrow boat and had started another chapter in our lives.

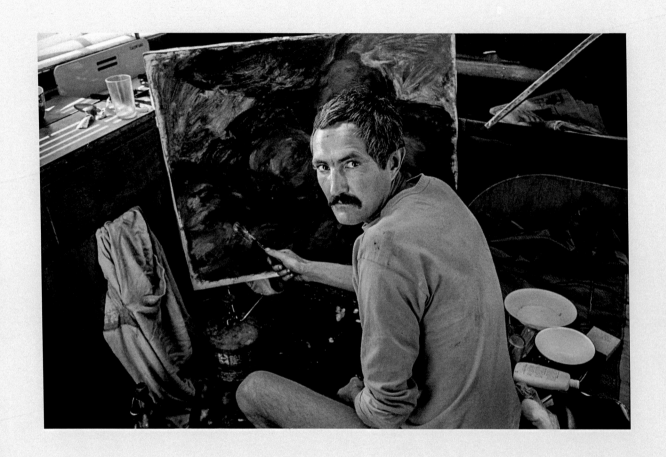

Bryan

My reasons for wanting to go on our road trip were rooted in my existentialist philosophy of life. I wanted to be free of all reasons to be anywhere. I wanted to travel to countries that had a more settled climate. I wanted to paint the landscape anytime I felt like it - early morning, late evening, and not be in a "studio", isolated from life, but be part of things. I wanted to be outside all the time. I didn't want to have to "go out" but already be there with paint and canvas.

To do this we needed to be self sufficient and to have with us all that we would ever need. I was lucky in having a lovely, equally free spirited companion. The children had a good start in life.

I still paint today, 50 years on - lots of still lives, usually objects rather than the fruit as in the paintings in the photographs. I also paint landscapes.

I have had a few exhibitions but recently I've just painted, gone my own way as usual. I think I have improved?!.

Life and art are inseparable to me.

Josephine

As the eldest I felt responsible and kept an eye on my younger brother and sister. I remember organising them and possibly ordering them around.

I was very independent and loved the cowboy boots that were given to me. I felt very proud in them and although they were two sizes too big, I treasured them. I was also very particular. I used to take every grain of sand off my towel before I would lie down on it.

We used to ride on the hammock behind the driver's seat and look out of the window - seeing great holes in the roads and car accidents. I was very wary when we drove at night and often tried to stay awake as I felt nervous and responsible again. The hammock fell down a couple of times when we went over bumps which was also quite unsettling. We had a transfer sticker on the lower bunk where Emma and I slept of a Hula girl playing a ukulele which I always thought was very glamorous.

One thing that always sticks in my mind is spending one time on the beach looking at ladies. I liked their make up , especially red lipstick (which I wear today) and their fashion. I also went along the beach asking them their names looking for someone else with the same name as me, Josephine. Even then I knew it was an unusual. I don't remember Bryan and Catherine working but they were always there. We ate well and we were free all day and I never remember being bored as I always kept myself busy as I do now.

Emma

I think we look like we belong to the travelling lifestyle - happy and relaxed. The outside world was our playground and our little blue van was our home. The excitement of different places, not knowing what to expect when you stepped out and then just running so freely, like children need to, was amazing fun. Life was simple. Our childhood was dreamlike. Our parents were there in the background - no school, childcare or pressure - just living day to day with that love and peace literally keeping us all together. Of course they worked, but when one was working the other one looked after us.

In the family portrait there is a little toy car. It was about the only toy we had. Its paint work was scratched and I think it was a Jaguar or a Daimler. It had little hard rubber wheels and we made tracks in the dry earth and sand with it.

I was not allowed near the cowboy boots as they were my sister's, an early indicator of her indomitable style.

It was coming to England where people gave you rules (in school especially) that the freedom we had had became apparent to me. It shocked me, from running bare foot on the sand to wearing shoes that felt suffocating. Fences, tarmac, orders, school, oppression and control - all these constraints that we had never experienced before made me realise what freedom we had had and how important it was for everyone to have nature and the benefits it gives to your personal strength. That's what life is all about for me.

Mason

Innocence and freedom!

A Moment in Time - SPAIN 1969

33

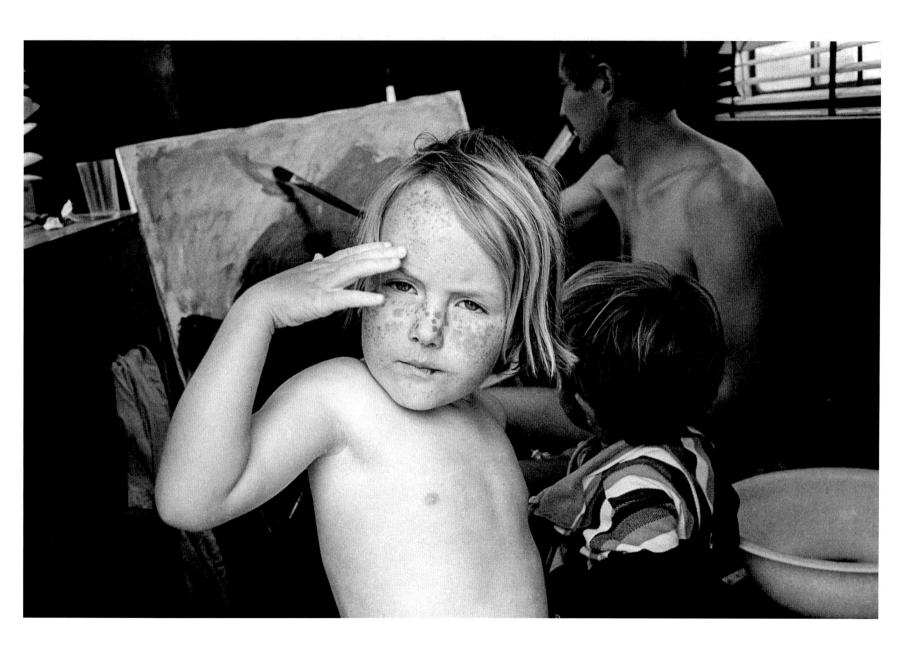

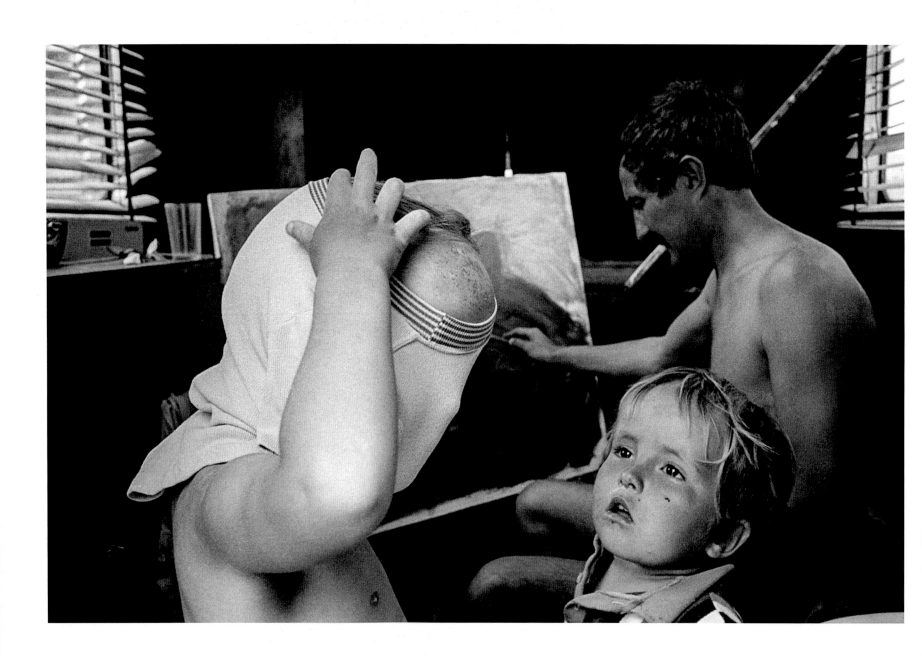

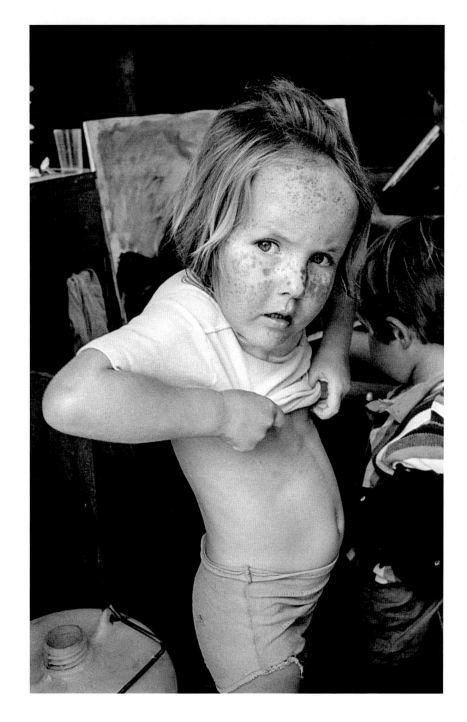

60

ACKNOWLEDGEMENTS

A big thank you to Andy Gregory, Steve Whale and Judy Harrison for helping speed along the completion of this book on the last leg of its journey.

My thanks to all the Whitfields.
Paul

A Moment in Time - SPAIN 1969

First Edition, August 2016

Paul Carter • Publishing

Southampton, SO19 9GD, UK

+44 (0)7718 793117, +44 (0)23 80 436191

paul@paulcarter-photographer.co.uk

Editors - Paul Carter , Emma Whitfield, Catherine Whitfield, Josephine Whitfield

Photographs by Paul Carter

Design by Paul Carter and the Whitfields

Distribution by **Paul Carter • Publishing**

All text copyright of the individual authors

All photographs copyright © Paul Carter

ISBN: 978-0-9929406-1-4

Printed in Great Britain by Printdomain